HUNGER

poems by

Erica Manto Paulson

Finishing Line Press
Georgetown, Kentucky

HUNGER

Copyright © 2021 by Erica Manto Paulson
ISBN 978-1-64662-582-6 First Edition
All rights reserved under International and Pan-American Copyright Conventions. No part of this book may be reproduced in any manner whatsoever without written permission from the publisher, except in the case of brief quotations embodied in critical articles and reviews.

ACKNOWLEDGMENTS

My appreciation to the editors of the journals and anthologies in which versions of the following poems have appeared:

Thimble Literary Magazine—"Midwifing Loss"
Adanna: Mothering in a Pandemic—"When Dairy Farmers Were Dumping Milk During the Pandemic"
The Dayton Anthology—"The Gift in the Parking Lot"
The Northern Appalachian Review—"Crossing the Edge in November"
"St. Anne's Hill After the Quarantine," chosen as the Dayton Metro Library 2020 poetry award winner and published in *Mock Turtle Zine*
Flights—"Three Little Stones" and "The Naming of Things"
The Cincinnati Poet Laureates' 2020 National Poetry Month project, *Postcards from the Pandemic*—"Pandemic in Early Spring"

Publisher: Leah Huete de Maines
Editor: Christen Kincaid
Cover Art: Carolyn Manto Cancelliere
Author Photo: Scott Paulson
Cover Design: Elizabeth Maines McCleavy

Order online: www.finishinglinepress.com
also available on amazon.com

Author inquiries and mail orders:
Finishing Line Press
PO Box 1626
Georgetown, Kentucky 40324
USA

Table of Contents

The Breastmilk Cure 1
First Memory 2
Hunger 3
Resilience 4
Three Little Stones 5
My Great-Grandmother Tells Me in a Dream to Write
    About Her Grief 6
First Birth in Four Sections 7
My Daughter Asks About the Border Wall 9
St. Anne's Hill, After the Quarantine 10
A Doula's Instructions for Starting Labor 11
Born At Home 12
Opposite Day 14
Just Wings 15
The Naming of Things 16
The Gift in the Parking Lot 17
Mom-Body 18
When I Heard Dairy Farmers Were Dumping Milk
    During the Pandemic 19
Forgiveness 20
Crossing the Edge in November 21
Harvesting Graveside Dandelion Greens 22
Litany to Our Lady of Destabilization 23
Midwifing Loss 24
The Last Thing is Also the First Thing 25
Your Doula Friend Talks to You in a Dream 26
After Birth 27
For the Young Mother Inside My Body 28
Pandemic in Early Spring 29
You Have 30

For my children and all who hunger

The Breastmilk Cure

I used to be able to squirt milk
from my breasts across the room.
It was my skill. The milk—
raw and full-fat, cream on top.
I put rolls of deliciousness
on my baby's thighs, cured
pink eye, pacified. My babies
slept like babies—milk drunk,
eyes rolling into the back
of their little heads—fed, clothed,
held, coddled, put down,
picked up, nursed again when
they were hungry, bored, tired,
happy, sad, over-my-shoulder
as acrobatic toddlers, under
my shirt, in a sling, skinned
knees, everywhere, every time,
my milk cured. Even me.

First Memory

Isolation
like a secret
swaddled
into blankets
unspiraled
when I lifted
baby sister
from the cradle
her tiny hands
gripping the air
in fists
while my naughty
heart raced and
my stomach
twisted into a ball
like the bedsheets
soiled and
tumultuous
inside the throb
of a washing machine,
off-kilter.
I am bad
I am bad
I am bad,
I covered her mouth
with small kisses
to muffle
her crying that never
reached our mother,
I only wanted
to hold her
close
to my chest
as though
she was my own.

Hunger

I had a nose ring my baby would touch
while he was at my breast—his little finger
pointing at the small white crystal on my nose
while he suckled, he was so proud
of his discovery, looking up as if to let me know
it was there, his eyes pouring into mine
and the milk I made for him dribbling out the corner
of his mouth—we were in such abundance.

Don't ever question your hunger in this world,
or whether the prophet lied when he said
to open your mouth wide and it will be filled
with good things—don't you know he too
stood like Abraham in the darkness,
staring into the depths of his aloneness,
the constellations glittering
on the face of the night sky, a billion stars
gazing back at him, his whole body
dripping with light.

Resilience

Some hearts
    when broken
        multiply.
Worms for instance and
        the eye of a potato
    that sprouts where gouged.
            Also cactus fruit
    if you cut it right
and
        a lizard's tail
although not a heart
when severed
will grow again.

Resilience is not always
    a conscious effort
like
        the bird who hides her nest on instinct
or
    the amount of times
        I have to tell you
I love you.
I love you.
I love you.

Three Little Stones

In my mind, I lift her whole body
into my arms like a bouquet
of flowers, my little girl in the red
wool coat with the pointed hood
pulled up over her soft brown curls,

she holds three little stones in her fist.
I remember everything about loving her—
especially how time slipped
through my fingers even as I held her

tightly in my arms, and how I can't recall
what it was to look into her face but
I do remember so clearly the little stones

and how she never wanted to put them down.

My Great-Grandmother Tells Me in a Dream to Write About Her Grief
For Peter, on the 76th Anniversary of D-Day

When I was your mother and you were at war,
your body was a pair of pants left crumpled
on the field. I picked them up and then

you were the egg yolk from breakfast scraped
from the plate, I wasn't hungry.

Every time I closed my eyes, you were my little boy
chasing his ball into the street while the war came
barreling down the road, intoxicated.

In Italian we say I miss you this way, mi manchi—
you are missing from me.

I have a place set for you at the dinner table
I brought to America, if you ever come back.
I don't know where home is, but I have this table.

It was the only thing on the boat with legs, still standing.

First Birth in Four Sections

1.

Just before they cut me open,
they said, as if I thought it mattered,
Don't worry—
you can still wear a bikini
when we're done with you,
no one will ever even know.

2.

I dreamt they rummaged
through every drawer of my body
to find her. I had only half
of every pair—one heart
where I should have two;
one lung, one kidney.
Everything a mess, my intestines
were a leg of jeans
hanging out a half-closed
drawer. When they reached
my womb, her little body
was neatly folded inside.

3.

When she learned the words,
I heard the story of her birth
the way she remembered,
> I was a mermaid
> swimming in your belly, mamma
> and the octopus stung me.

4.

She stopped crying when
they brought her near me.
My arms still tied to the table—
we held each other anyways.

My Daughter Asks About the Border Wall

Chances are, we are dying. There's no more
real food to eat. The water is contaminated.
We are in airplanes traveling for work
more than we are in our bodies.
We teach our children to stop crying
when we leave them and reward them
for learning to sit still and sleep alone.

Today my daughter asked—what happens
to the babies who are pulled from their mothers
at the border wall? When I asked, she said
what she meant is, how do they get the milk
from the mothers' breasts to the babies?
Who feeds them?

St. Anne's Hill, After the Quarantine
Dayton, Ohio 2019

I learned to not take things for granted by feeding horses when I was
   very young.
This is especially important to me now when we are skeptical of
   everything,
having known so many bits and bridles that have pulled us by our teeth
during these months of staying distant from your body; mine.

If we will ever hold each other again on the hill where the tall grasses
   touch
the stone wall like a painting, we must stand still like the horses, who
   were here,
in this valley, a thousand years before us, and let the wind carry our
   scent to where
we find each other drinking coffee in the sunlight of the old violin
   maker's workshop.

I'd like to think if I hold out my palm, flat like a plate and balance the
   round, beautiful
fruit that has ripened from all we have lost, you will come to me. And
   standing like
creatures in a pasture, nuzzling over the fence, we will embrace this
   new longing,
distant though we may have become for a time.

A Doula's Instructions for Starting Labor

She should make love
but only if she wants it; tell her
an orgasm will help start the labor.
Wait until the moon is full or
when a storm is coming. Try
Cotton Root Bark
in the morning: 2 droppers
every 15 minutes for 4 hours
under the tongue and strip
the membranes. Borage oil
by mouth and on her cervix,
she can rub it in. Black Cohosh
to stimulate blood circulation,
Blue is an oxytocic.
If nothing happens, sing to her.
Bathe her. Stimulate her
nipples. Wrap her in a blanket.
You are speaking to the baby
through the medium of the mother's body.
It's hard to want to leave the womb.
Tell her, it's ok to be born.

Born at Home

1.

First Stage

we were together all day
                  there were eggs
for breakfast and orange juice
too sweet to drink
        I walked and walked
throughout a day
        longer than any of the others
                I had carried you—both of us,
in a body more yours
than mine then, I was not as eager
        to let you go
as with the others,
holding on to something, but
I didn't know what.

2.

Second Stage

wet curls over fontanelles
        like spring moss
               on a rock,
your head at a full
        crown,
                I cried
when your shoulders
rotated inside me,
        the unlocking
               of our bodies
        ruptured membranes,
                waters broken
you emerged

       and it was called birth
when you took that piece of the atmosphere
       in a breath
alive
             for the first time—
in your own body.

3.

Third Stage

       every time
a baby
is born,
       we start over—
             we are opened,
       we close
the world expands again.

Opposite Day

You be
the mamma,
      make
yourself
into
      a castle
           where we can live
a mountain
a hollowed tree
a river
      who is always moving
a whale
      who has
    an ocean
        inside
           the ocean
of her body
        a boulder
           be unmoved
    be a bee
that finds the petals
        back bending
                from the center
          of the flower
    the way I do
like this,
like this.

Just Wings

I wanted to hang them in the living room—two heavy angel wings carved from a single block of wood that a woman had given to me for attending her birth, I think her husband made them.
I wanted it to look like the angel Gabriel had just walked in our house and hung his wings on a hook right next to his umbrella, as though it were the most normal thing, but it didn't look right.

I moved them over near the kitchen sink, but that didn't work; then moved again descending along the stairs until one of my children (who had been watching me with those wings) asked why would anyone
> want to hang dead angel wings
> on a wall
> like they were a deer head
>
> and I said, Well that's not right-
> we have the baby Jesus on a cross
> and Mary and even St. Luke
> the Healer

but they didn't buy it.

I took them down and put the wings in the trunk of my car where they were forgotten until I was driving around town with my littlest boy—the windows were down and I could see him in my rearview mirror, a halo of sunshine around the fawn of his little body, curled up in the back seat. His soft, downy hair tousled by the breeze coming in the open window and he was smiling to himself, he was so light, he could have floated out the back window, and as I'm watching him, I realize I'm straying off the center of the road, so I pull back sharp on the wheel, and I hear the clunking of those wings in the back, but I've forgotten that they were there so I say abruptly,
> What was that?

and he looks over his shoulder then turns back to me, unmoved, and says,
> Nothing;
> just the wings.

The Naming of Things

A repetition of sound
becomes the utterance
that becomes a word
for a red feathered creature
my baby has discovered
in a fir tree
where it sits inside the branches,
shrouded with pine needles
and snow.

Bird

I say aloud
when he points his little finger
at what quietly observes him
from within the tree.

Bird

I say again,
crouching down beside him,
mesmerized at the way
his blue eyes pull everything in
while the red bird
holds his gaze within the branches.

We must name these things
for each other—the wild creatures
called love, need, loss.

I will tell you what it is
when you see your red heart
flitting in front of you
on the branches,
and how your eyes will sparkle
even as it flies away.

The Gift in the Parking Lot

The vampire cartoon drawing
that said I love you more
than all the flowers
on what would be the last day
he would ever run towards me
after school, flinging himself
at me like a wild dragon—
all wide eyed
and fire breathing
while the other children
walked to their parents
in the ordinary way.
Catching him, barely
again, I laughed and said
you're getting too big
and pulling me in
like a secret he whispered
you still catch me—
breathing in my scent,
waving the vampire drawing
in his hand
like a banner.

Mom-Body

"Mother and child are engaged in a silent chemical conversation throughout pregnancy, with bits of genetic material and cells passing not only from mother to child but also from child to mother. Scientists increasingly think these silent signals from the fetus may influence a mother's risk of cancer, rheumatoid arthritis and other diseases, even decades after she has given birth." —Scientific American, April 30, 2010

In case you needed proof
that your heart will never
be the same, you should know
that coiled, stem-rich strands
of your child's DNA
stayed behind when she left
your mom-body.

The streaked white marks
on your skin are battle wounds,
claim them. And where your vagina
was stretched beyond
its capabilities, you became

a fire-breathing goat of a woman,

a genetic chimera with a reservoir
for your child's cells, coiled serpent-like
inside your body, ready to heal.

You are a legendary beast
made from different animals—an omen
for what happens when you truly break
down and your mom-body tries to give up.

This is what I am trying to say: listen—
you are more than skin.

When I Heard Dairy Farmers Were Dumping Milk During the Pandemic

After my daughter was born, I dumped bottles of my breastmilk
down the kitchen sink after they had soured, forgotten on the
     countertop
by my newly postpartum, sleep-deprived brain. All of that milk
I made within the weariness of my new mother-body—gone.

I cried, it was the only thing in abundance at a time when nothing
felt like it was enough.

I used to walk the halls with her for hours while she mourned the
     womb,
not wanting her to be alone in whatever grief accompanied her.
At seventeen, she is a young woman herself now, yet still the same
oracle of a girl, weighted by the gravity of things.

I want to tell her in this poem how, by loving her, she saved my life.
Mothers holding daughters holding mothers—wrapping arms around
those young women pumping their breasts for their babies every hour,
with enough for both of them to live.

Forgiveness

There must have been a time
when my mother understood the darkness,
the way she would burn at both ends
so that we could have her light.

Yesterday, I thought I finally understood
how she survived her alcoholic father,
how he never erased her with his drinking,
but I couldn't say it—I'm not yet ready to forgive.

But today, I thought of my mother
when my Lenten roses burst into bloom—pink fire,
it stood in the barrenness
of my early spring garden like a burning bush
and I leaned close to hear if any god
would speak but like all things holy, it knew silence
was the only way to get through.

And as I began to pull at the dead branches
from last year's roses, their leaves
still sucking energy from the roots, I saw my mother
when she was a little girl—she was laughing,
holding the roses in her hand while the sun
was setting behind her, the beams so blinding
that she disappeared into the fullness of light.

Crossing the Edge in November

Driving across the big waters between Ohio and Kentucky,
a semi-truck crammed full of young turkeys pulled in front of me—
a hundred or more beautiful birds stacked one on top of the other
in crates across the bed of the truck. You can imagine my shame,

it being almost Thanksgiving, I knew where they were going
and I couldn't help but notice newly flecked, brown feathers
just starting to come in under the downy white covering their bodies,
the blue gobbler of the males was beginning to protrude along
their necks—they were just old enough to be afraid. At some point,

whether you try to avoid it or not, you will be on the edge
of young and afraid, and you will see the body you crammed yourself into
was the vehicle that carried you across the midlife line of the only
living you had ever known. It's time to break free now, leave that shell

on the banquet table the world will feast upon, you know their hunger.
Become the body of grace and of truth. Be kind to yourself, like earth and sky,
be like the river you had only ever crossed over, back and forth so many times,
until now when you are submerged in the place where the lines
between things are not so clear—in the thin places where there is no sign
that says welcome, you are home and you are leaving, goodbye.

Harvesting Graveside Dandelion Greens

The best dandelion greens were from the cemetery
where my uncle would cull them along the winding dirt path
of Our Lady of Mt. Carmel Cemetery. Often,
he strayed off the main road on his way home from the factory,

searching for the thickest, ruffled fronds—the ones dense
with chlorophyll, growing where no shoe had trampled them.
The plants with the deepest tap roots went as far as to touch
his father's coffin and the sisters, Louisa and Carmencita,
where they slept together, peaceful in darkness of earth.

Bursting through the door with a bouquet of greens,
just before his mother was beginning to grow impatient, her pots
hissing from every corner of the stove, he kissed her gently
on the top of her head before walking to the sink and rinsing the leaves,
whistling to himself as the dirt disappeared down the drain.

Litany to Our Lady of Destabilization
Arc of Appalachia, Adams County, Ohio

As unto the tourists at the caves
in the Rock Run Wilderness
restored after eighty years
of continuous fluorescent light,

forgive us—

for park gift shops selling
lucky crystals and
packs of gum, our
relentless pursuit of light,
for how we of little faith thrust
our hand into the wound
of the world
again and again
just to know it is real.

Ground water, salamander,
isopod, moss—forgive us
for the way our touch erases.

At the Chalet Nivale,
the snow trillium
are beginning to bloom
just as the frost is ending.

Restore us to the darkness
where we were formed, that
penetrating stem of desire,
how it pushes through
the clay, blooms
in full crown.

Midwifing Loss

A pregnant mother lost a baby at fourteen weeks
and buried the fetus behind a woodpile in her backyard.
Before that, she asked if I would see his small body
inside a blue ceramic bowl in her fridge and how
the baby's arm moved at the elbow hinge when
she touched him. He had a torso and legs and two palms
that would have clenched into fists when he cried.

Who can bear the shape of loss delivered
in a paralyzing gaze and all the ways it would have looked
like you? From the small cold mouth of survival, we hinge
at the joint and move. Let us remember how
we would have held on; where we would have loved.

The Last Thing Is Also the First Thing

The first thing is that none of us knew what to do with dying.
Your mother was hard to understand—was she thirsty?
Did her head hurt to sit that way? Should we move her?

The next thing is that she needed you to leave. Once, when
you went outside she asked if she was dying and I didn't know what to
say.

I thought death would be more noble and grand, but
it looked like the mask of a little girl covering her face—
she was frightened and small.

They say the living need help with letting go, but I saw your mother
fight like a fish on dry ground—her eyes fixed, her mouth opening
and closing to cup any amount of air into her lungs,

she wasn't holding on, she was holding your hand like a rosary
while she dangled over death, her body, a prayer and each finger
on your hand—a decade of longing and thanksgiving, both.

And the last thing your mother saw before she died was
the day you were born. I saw her kissing your fingers and counting
your toes the way every mother does, now and at the hour of our
deaths.

Your Doula Friend Talks to You in a Dream

I had a dream last night
where you decided to have a baby.
      You said, like Sarah and Abraham,
it wasn't too late, there was still a way.

All you wanted to know
      from me
was, why not numb the pain of birth?
      You had already thought
about all the other things.

I thought I understood you when I said—
      find a surrogate,
          let someone else do the pain for you.
You're old to be a mother,
it will hurt, the way they treat you.

You said that I didn't understand.
You said,
      I'm not afraid.

After Birth

A midwife reads between the veins
of your afterbirth and notes where
the membranes shredded, likely
from your diet of cheese curls
and the crusts of your toddler's leftover
peanut butter and jelly sandwiches.

Her hands observe the thin, long shape
which is more muscle—flank
like steak, and not the usual large,
meaty organ. She notes it has
an extra lobe, which grew later in pregnancy
when it crept over the uterine lining
in an attempt to give more
than you could give to the baby.

She sees love in three vessels
of the umbilicus, but mostly from your children,
which is not enough for any woman.

Where your body pulled calcium from
your teeth and pumped water from your muscles,
your hair falls at the follicle like the feathers
of a molting bird. Your afterbirth, once

warm and pulsating, cools inside a metal
bowl—it is finished now, let it go.
You will sustain life again.

For the Young Mother Inside My Body

Scattered seed opens green tendrils,
pushing upwards through softening spring mud.

Rippled ribbons of creeks run like tears
down the face of an open field

where the young mother inside my body
tries to stand still.

The baby, once perched on the brim
of my pelvic bowl, kicking his dimpled legs

back and forth, delighted, has grown.
Now even my bones don't know

where that mother stands or how she fits
inside my aging skin. This body is all

I have ever known of being a woman—a home,
never empty. Now the space inside widens

like the rings in trees where squirrels hide nests
as they have done for a thousand seasons and

will for a thousand more. Every petal of the day lily
that opens, browns before it falls from the stem

and returns to earth, heavy in the weight of full bloom.

Pandemic in Early Spring

We have to wear gloves when we touch,
the virus must be everywhere and nothing
feels real—the apples at the grocery store,
the keypad at the bank, door handles,
shopping cart, the coffee cup I fill
and refill at the gas station—they all feel
the same, but the daffodils are coming up anyways,
straight through the newly softened ground
like loyal soldiers—green and determined.

Yesterday I thought, finally we are done
with snow forever, then it snowed harder
than it had all winter and I felt sad.
It's the only way I know people are dying.

I never realized how much I listen through touch
until I couldn't hear your fingerprints
on the pages of these lines,
which made me think of the daffodils and
how they are disturbed only by the thawing
of the ground as though it is their calling,
as though they've been waiting all their life
to hear: rain, sunlight, bee, cloud, wind.

You Have

the vespers
of the setting sun
sinking
behind the barn
and
the calico cat
giving
herself a bath
on the broken
windowsill,
red lilies
of the field
bowing
their heads
in wind or
in stillness,

and the dirt path
is worn through
the tall grass,
and the creek
is high,
and your lover's breath
blue
and ubiquitous
as the cornflower.

In August
after the haying
the horse
will stamp her foot
while
you hitch her
to the wagon.

She wants
to take you
home.

ABOUT THE COVER ART

The cover art was created especially for this chapbook by my sister and native Cincinnati artist, Carolyn Manto Cancelliere. Carolyn's art is a visual poem about the human experience that often tells a story of what lies below the surface of the skin. Her work has been the recipient of numerous awards and honors and her commissions include a bronze sculpture for the lobby of the National Underground Railroad Freedom Center (Cincinnati, Ohio) and a bronze sculpture for the Black Brigade Monument in Smale Park commissioned by the Cincinnati Park Board Registry. Carolyn and I come from an Italian-American family and our heritage is very influential in our work. The drawing for Hunger is based on fountains in Italy depicting lactating nereids, sirens, and goddesses where Nature is represented as a lactating woman. These mythological characters were popular icons for protection, regeneration, and fertility in the 16th century. Some believe breastmilk also symbolizes wisdom, in which the breast is represented as an inexhaustible source.

Additional Acknowledgments

An abundance of gratitude to Pauletta Hansel, my teacher and poet-midwife, who attended to me in the birthing of these poems and the crafting of this book, with mercy and grace. Many thanks to the poets from "Draft to Craft" and the Thomas More Creative Vision writing program, especially Roberta Schultz, Richard Westheimer, Kris Gillis, and Ellen Austin-Li for their editing advice and support. I am also exceedingly grateful for the Wright Poets, especially David Lee Garrison who has been an early advocate of my work and whose last-minute editing advice made all the difference, Kathy Austin, Betsy Hughes, Elizabeth Schmidt and all poets who have supported and written alongside me—we hunger together.

A depth of gratitude to my sister, Carolyn Manto Cancelliere, for creating the cover art for this book and to all my family, to my children who are often also my teachers, and especially to my husband, Scott—you were always with me.

A native Ohioan, **Erica Manto Paulson** finds inspiration for her poetry in the fertile fields of her home state, drawing on a deep connection to the surrounding world and the "holy ordinary" of everyday life. Erica holds a BFA in Creative Writing from Bowling Green State University and is also a certified doula, midwife assistant, and childbirth educator. In 2006 she started one of Cincinnati's first doula agencies and became the president of the Cincinnati Area Doula Society and the first Ohio faculty doula trainer for CAPPA International before retiring in 2017.

During a significant period of awakening into the second-half of her life, Erica rediscovered poetry (and her voice) at a poetry workshop led by Pauletta Hansel (Cincinnati's first poet laureate). A familiar face in the Dayton & Cincinnati area poetry groups, Erica's poetry brings the reader into the intimate spaces of human triumphs and sufferings. Her poetry has appeared in *Thimble Literary Magazine, The Northern Appalachian Review, Adanna Literary Journal, The Dayton Anthology,* and *Mock Turtle Zine* among others and has been featured on local NPR's poetry spotlight, "Conrad's Corner." Erica lives in Dayton with her husband and their beautifully blended brood of seven children.

www.ingramcontent.com/pod-product-compliance
Lightning Source LLC
LaVergne TN
LVHW041555070426
835507LV00011B/1093